We will fly higher

Palewell Press

We will fly higher

*Poems by Parwana Amiri
Autumn 2020-Autumn 2021*

We will fly higher

First edition 2022 from Palewell Press, www.palewellpress.co.uk

Printed and bound in the UK

ISBN 978-1-911587-64-4

All Rights Reserved. Copyright © 2022 Parwana Amiri. No part of this publication may be reproduced or transmitted in any form or by any means, without permission in writing from the author. The right of Parwana Amiri to be identified as the author of this work has been asserted by her in accordance with the Copyright, Designs and Patents Act 1988

The cover design is Copyright © 2022 Camilla Reeve
The front cover illustration is Copyright © 2022 Alexandra Nikolova (Ål Nik).
The back cover photo of Parwana Amiri is Copyright © 2022 Judith Buethe.

A CIP catalogue record for this title is available from the British Library.

Acknowledgements

All I thank is from my Allah, for granting me the natural power to write poems in my non-mother language.

Thank you for not letting me get lost in this journey. Thanks for appearing in the dark sky of my life to let me see my way.

A fist of love and thanks to "brush and bow" for opening the door to share my poems with.

A big mountain of thanks to Roshan De Stone for trusting in my poetry voice.

A deep valley of thanks to Beryl de Stone for being in my life as a moon, in this dismal night and has kept my literary life bright, shining.

A warm, wavy ocean of thanks to Sappho Haralambous and who has always been a great supporter in sharpening this soft sword of mine.

A galaxy of thanks to Alex Nik, for the cover illustration.

Shiny, tiny stars of thanks to Alex Fusco and Gavin D'Costa who appeared in the way of my writings with suggestions and comments about each word and line I have written.

A heart of thanks to the strength of all displaced people, specially displaced females, who have inspired me to write this collection. I have evolved all your pains and am sending this cover to the world to let your pains get healed.

Warm thanks to Palewell Press, for building this bridge among me, and you.

Keep us and our words in your heart, for that sea has swallowed us in its womb.

Contents

Introduction	2
We are burning	4
How easy you…we	5
It needs courage	6
We were in distress	8
In this fire	10
Your Eyes Bother Us	12
Every night…Before sleep	14
I spoke with her eyes	15
In front of my eyes	16
You can stay silent but…	18
Where Can We Find Freedom?	20
In the camps…	22
I swear that I will never stay silent	24
You miss me!	26
Like the light at the end of the tunnel	28
Greetings to nature	30
Butterfly and Nature	31
Up to Down	32
Now, it is you…and…they	34
My body is covered, what about your eyes	36
Don't look at me like that	37
Carrying the Sun	38
The Bride of Snow	39
Keep me Drugged	40

14 days at home	42
When Schools Reopened	44
Never give up!	46
This never-ending struggle	48
A conversation from behind the walls	50
My homeland	52
Our Flag	54
One Nation	56
The Displaced	57
Parwana Amiri – Biography	60

Sometimes words need a rhythm to find their way and make the revolution in your mind, that is when my poetry forms!

Parwana Amiri 2022

Introduction

There is a pain, a strength, so much bravery, a smile and a sparkle that is asleep in these poems, I hug all of them and send them to you.

When Moria camp burned down and a mother lost her child, I felt a smoke in the words I wanted to express, so I wrote my first poem in Ritsona refugee camp "We are burning". I shared it with the public and they called it a "poem".

I had never known about the literary structure of English poetry as a Dari speaker, but this nomination from Public encouraged me, inspired me to feel more free in expressing all my complex thoughts in poems.

Poetry opened her arm to my untold words, while I knew nothing about English poetry. Sometimes your feelings are much more complicated or clear to write in prefixes, that is when my poems are born from the belly of my heart.

I have felt like becoming a mother by publishing each poem, each with a specific scene behind. Like a tree who gives fruits which some of them are bitter, or a caterpillar who becomes butterflies.

"We" as refugees, displaced people, people without documents, minorities, third nation citizens have been marginalized in a thousand different ways. We want to strive, but not to survive.

"The displaced" tells about the beauty of our journey by striving, fighting, struggling, demanding and being loud. We will never let the borders, the camps, detention centres and barbed wires silence our words, "We will fly higher" as we share our words in art, music, literature and protests, and believe that you will share them from heart to heart, generation to generation, to keep this fire of loudness and strength lit forever.

Who can express us better than ourselves? I wanted to write these poems to bring alive our injuries and wounds and let the world not forget the injustice we had been through. Verse by verse, line by line and spaces among the lines are part of our souls, that would spy inside us.

"We will fly higher" and will not be crushed upon the earth. Still more flowers to blossom, more golden leaves to fall and shells to be washed on the shore. I am holding your hand to welcome you to our world. We are not alone in these poems.

We are burning

It's not to mark the date!
It's to raise the alarm!
The fire has burned our homes.
The fire has burned our schools.
The fire has burned our hospitals.
The fire has burned our dreams.
We are burning.
We search for your eyes.
You have turned them away.
You have hidden your faces.
Who is the criminal? Not the fire, for sure!
Who shall pay for the life of the burned child?
Who shall answer the mother, never to touch her child again?
Who can answer?
Who dares imagine the screams of the baby burning?
The baby was crying…
Was crying, was crying…
The baby was burning, a bundle of coal left.
Where are those who cursed us?
Those afraid we threatened their wealth?
Come on and see!
Do you dare to look at this scene?
Better avert your eyes.
Hide and lock yourselves in your homes!
We are silent so that you hear us.

Author's Footnote: This poem was written, with all respect and love to the family of the young child who lost his life, burning in the fire accident in Moria Lesvos at the beginning of 2020. 23/08/2020

How easy you…we

How easy you left us behind
How hard we continued the way
How easy you faded our lives
How hard we stayed displayed
How easy you suffocated our voices
How hard we broke the silence
How easy you called us a danger
How hard we proved our peace
How easy you counted our deaths
How hard we lost our beloved ones
How easy you called us terrorists
How hard we live with terror
How easy you left us in darknesses
How hard we found lights for our way
How easy you thought us most greedy
How hard we proved being simply refugees
How easy you hid and trapped us
How hard we lived your hells and prisons
How easy you left us in the past
How hard we struggle with present
How easy you sleep in sweet dreams
How hard we live in nightmares
How easy you threaten to divide us
How hard we prove being united
How easy you burned our dreams
How hard we draw new dreams
How easy you left us in prison
How hard we must break the chains

Author's Footnote: *At every step of the refugees' journey – from its beginning to the moment they get recognized and afterwards, from the first border they pass, till the last shelter they receive – they must be strong to deal with discrimination and other challenges. 03/05/2020*

It needs courage

It needs courage to build a school!
It needs courage to touch children's hearts!
It needs courage to welcome homelessness!
It needs courage to stand with us in one line!
It needs courage to open an educational house!
It needs courage to give hope for hopelessness!
It needs courage to give pens to those that have never touched a pen before!
It needs courage to paint the black and white world of the wounded!
It needs courage to advocate from silences!
It needs courage to give shelter to others!
It needs courage to stay human!
It needs courage!
It needs courage!
BECAUSE ….
It's easy to destroy!
It's easy to break hearts!
It's easy to shout at the silenced!
It's easy to close your eyes on truths!
It's easy to hurt those who have been hurt many times!
It's easy to set aside!
It's easy to show your power against weaknesses!
It's easy!
It's easy!

But, we will never give up!
We will build again, stronger than before!
We will help again, more committed than before!
We will bring happiness and stay happy, happier than before!
We will make islands free

Author's Footnote: *Solidarity and respect to those who lost their school in the fire attack against one of the refugee support centers in Lesvos. The attack was carried out by racist people on the island: whose slogan was "reclaiming the islands." 18/09/2020*

We were in distress

On a dark scary night
As the moon was smiling
In the middle of the sea
We were in distress

My mother was crying
Scared for us all
In that angry rough sea
We were in distress

Time was passing slowly
Seconds were counted
Danger was alerting us
We were in distress

Stars were sparkling
Water was all around
Babies were all crying
We were in distress

Thousands of dreams in the sea
Many people's courage was put to the test
To reach safety, crossing the sea
We were in distress

Some holes in our rubber dinghy
Let the water in slowly
We took both our shoes off
We were in distress

We searched for something
Nothing around to
Throw the water out of the dinghy
We were in distress

Our hearts were pulsing hard
Our eyes were getting wet
We were sinking
We were in distress

The final moments were upon us
We reached the shore
Exhausted, alone, distressed
We reached Europe

Author's Footnote: *I like the power of poetry to express the scenes I have experienced as a refugee. In this poem I recall being with other refugees in a rubber dinghy, trying to reach Europe. In our last effort to cross the Aegean Sea, there were many people in one boat and it was a dangerous, terrifying night. The dinghy was taking on water and we were trying to bail it out. As you read this poem, remember those who are still trying to pass borders and putting their lives at risk in a rubber boat with the aim of reaching safety. 25/09/2020*

In this fire

It does not only burn into ashes
It does not only destroy
It does not only kill

A fire....

It can make light to see
It can guide in the darkness
It can warm in the cold

A fire....

A candle needs the fire
A meal needs the fire
To start up, to turn on, to show out

But we don't need the fire
We have been burning a long time
We don't need the fire
We don't hold a candle in our night

In this fire....
We lost our hopes
We lost our tents, our new homes
Here in this host country, in its camps
As we did in our country that we fled

In this fire....
In Moria, in Samos, in Chios
In Refugee camps around Greece
We have been burning silently
Subjugated, without dignity

In this fire....
Tens of us have burned
Changed to bundles of coal
No raised voices, no closed fists
Silence has never been a solution

After this fire....
We can find, we can move
We can want, we can raise
our heads, our fists and our voice
Asking for "freedom of movement"

Author's Footnote: *This poem focuses on fire, which has been a strong reason for vulnerability for a long time in all refugee camps, especially in the overcrowded Moria camp.* 24/10/2020

Your Eyes Bother Us

It is not a drama film
We are not actors
Don't be spectators
Your eyes bother us!

Trees are our shelter
The earth is our floor
This is a real scene
Your eyes bother us!

Violence and humiliation
Scorn and repression
Don't see us as criminals
Your eyes bother us!

Your support is admirable
But, don't take our pictures
The lenses, your eyes
Your eyes bother us!

On the roads, passengers
In the tents, tourists
In war, among soldiers
Your eyes bother us!

Not the eyes, only hearts
Not the eyes, only thoughts
Not the eyes, only glances
Those eyes bother us!

(Full of respect for all solidarity people who were always there to help us, this poem is only for those who couldn't change their perspective about us)

To survive, to breathe
To achieve our goals
Not to stay in darkness
We struggled in Greece

Author's Footnote: *While respecting the solidarity of those who were always there to help us, this poem is addressed to the people who couldn't change their perspective about refugees. 03/10/2020*

Every night…Before sleep

Every night, silently
Every night, lonely
I dress my harsh realities
In dreams
Every night, with my pen
Every night, with my words
I hug my dreams
I review my story
Every night, before sleep
Every night, when all sleep
In my silence, with myself
I build with my words
A new world
In my world, home is for all
in my world, school is a right
In my world, you have peace
In my world, war is banned
In my world, the world is for all
Sun is mom, moon dad
Mother earth is a planet for all
But
When I close my eyes
In dreams, as in reality,
I live nightmares ……

Author's Footnote: *This poem expresses feelings I cannot share elsewhere, feelings I have every night, thinking about the days passing and my future in this world, in which I cannot find my dreams. Like many youths and children, I make my dreams in a world that I want to live in, a dream world in which borders do not exist.*

I spoke with her eyes

She was silent but thoughtful
She was alone but brave
Full of words, but stifled, muted
I spoke with her eyes

A sparkle illuminated her eyes
A faded bloom rested on her lips
Loud was her pulsing heart
I spoke with her eyes

Her repressed soul was lifted
Holding onto her dreams
Sitting down in a **summer** tent
I spoke with her eyes

Many were her sore pains
Many the injures in her young soul
Screaming for right and justice
I spoke with her eyes

I spoke with her eyes
I read her story and trials
A lost family…crossing the borders
She was a refugees girl

Author's Footnote: *There was a girl I saw in Moria Refugee Camp who seemed different from the other girls, unable to trust anyone. After some months of being in our neighborhood, she managed to speak with others and we came to understand that she had lost her entire family during their journey to Greece. This poem is inspired by her and thousands of refugees like us who faced the same trials. 11/10/2020*

In front of my eyes

Everything is burning
Everyone is fleeing
Children are crying
I do not know what to do

In front of my eyes...
Tents collapse into ashes
Nothing remains sound
Smoke invades the eyes
Nothing exists but fire

In front of my eyes...
Babies are screaming,
Are they burning?
No one can help another
Each after his own survival

In front of my eyes...
Everyone is seeking water
Not a drop to be found
Some with bags or blankets
Cling their children in their embrace

In front of my eyes...
A baby clutches her doll
To keep it safe
She may play with it later
No one knows her world

In front of my eyes...
A mother is sobbing
Screaming for her lost boy in Moria
No one reaches her, no one helps
No one asks her — how she feels

In front of my eyes...
I can stay no longer
I could be one of them, among them
If I would be a refugee, in prison
I got lucky, should I not hold their hands?

In front of the world's eyes...
Open your eyes, these are real scenes
You, too, could be one of them
Don't blame; stay, help!
You don't know what a "refugee" means

Author's Footnote: *Conditions for refugees in the new Moria Cmp were terrifying and inhumane, but it should be forgotten that refugees in camps like Moria have been burning for years. This poem was written from the viewpoint of someone who witnessed what happened to people; with the hope that readers will search for solutions to the current situation;.and to express solidarity with people there. 01/11/2020*

You can stay silent, but…

If we are burning, among the fire
If we are sinking, in the heavy rains
If we are fading, in enclosed camps
If we are waiting, for an unclear time
You can stay silent!

If we are children, with thousands of dreams
If we are young girls, hoping to become free
If we have male voice, full of power in veins
If we are pushed to stay in downright nights
You can stay silent!

If we leave our tents, when they burn down
If we live in shelters, even they sink under mud
If our children are starving, with no milk or food
If we are in temporary prisons, without freedom
You can stay silent!

If there is no light, in the darkness of our nights
If there is no water, when we are quarantined
If we must stay in lines, with thousands of people
If we must follow the injustices rules and laws
You can stay silent!

You can stay silent, but imagine yourself, if
You were one of us, here in the camps
Listen our voice, even if it is repressed
You can stay silent, but do not pretend
You do not hear us, while we are calling "'help"

Author's Footnote: *After the second fire attack on Moria camp, every single tent had burnt down and all the residents had to stay on the streets. Conditions became really horrible for all, but few stood up for their rights. This silence about the conditions of those more vulnerable than us, those who become shelter-less after each accident in refugee camps screams to be written about, so that readers see our reality, and decide whether to keep silent in the face of our sufferings. 07/12/2020*

Where Can We Find Freedom?

Our long-term life in prison
From detentions to ghettos
With no self-determination
Where can we find freedom?

Everywhere are stop signs
Telling we are limited
Suffocated and repressed
Where can we find freedom?

Absence of smiles from faces
Privation of pens from hands
Silence was chosen to survive
Where can we find freedom?

Protest is banned
But tear gas allowed
And we must just absorb it
Where can we find freedom?

We were oppressed in our lands
We were depressed crossing borders
With no right to ask, to act
Where can we find freedom?

To pass borders, to find freedom
With our mothers on dark nights
Among deserts with no water
Where can we find freedom?

Our lands were our prison
Our homes were our cells
Our schools were captured
Where can we find freedom?

After trials, after failures
Stressed, afraid, anxious
We reached Moria, a hell
Where can we find freedom?

Where can we find freedom?
For us, refugees, migrants
Can freedom exist?
With all our might we shall fight for it.

Author's Footnote: *This poem is inspired by the feelings that come from being enclosed in refugee camps, denied freedom of speech or movement, but instead repressed by rules.*

In the camps…

We are limited and repressed
We are enclosed and depressed
In makeshift summer tents
We are fading in Greek camps

In the summer, it is like hell
In the winter, we live on mud
We are exposed to cold, to wind
Without even warm clothes

Our children, while playing
Their shoes sink into
Mud and sewage water
This condition is suffocating

Girls are trapped in the tents
Their voices, their faces
Among wolves leering, in fear
For their integrity and honour

But, how long will we be here?
How long should we suffer?
With these little children
How long will we live in war?

In the camps, with no peace
Dignity, honour or respect
Far from our loved ones
If only we could be evacuated!

Author's Footnote: *I suffered since the first day I arrived in Greece, not only from the physical conditions, but the situation's emotional impact on me was intolerable. This poem addresses all aspects of the refugees' problems in the camp: especially those of girls, women, children, and all vulnerable people.* 05/01/2021

I swear that I will never stay silent

I swear to the smiles of displaced children
I swear to the tears of injured mothers
I swear to the millions of hidden dreams
That I will never stay silent!

I swear to the death borders, we passed
I swear to our beloved ones we lost
I swear to the dark windy nights, in fear
That I will never stay silent!

I swear to my shed tears, hopeless
I swear to my tired pen, every night
I swear to my hopes that are trapped
That I will never stay silent!

I swear to our black and white world
I swear to our blood written "Help"
I swear to our hopes, that surround us
That I will never stay silent!

I swear to our days, which do not pass
I swear to our pains, which are not cured
I swear to our beloved ones, who have died
That I will never stay silent!

I swear to our repressed voices,
I swear to our fading faces
I swear to our trapped rights
That I will never stay silent!

I swear to the fullness of my dream
I swear to the crashing of those dreams
I swear to the small dinghy in the sea
That I will never stay silent!

I swear to the blood of my brother
To the hijab of my sister "Farkhonda"
To the broken heart of Rahid's mother
To the closed fists of my homeland's fathers
To the sunny days in refugee camps, in Greece
To the burning tents in Moria, Samos, Khios
To the naked sculptures in Bosnia's border
To the girls married at a young age
To the violence against women
To the gray world of the wounded
To the destroyed hospitals and schools.
To the students who die under desks
I will never rest silent

Author's Footnote: *Silence has never been a solution. Because of the work I do, I have been exposed to many questions, challenges and problems. But these have never been an obstacle as they helped me to develop. Exposing my emotions in the face of suffering has allowed me to grow my resilience and speak out against the bombing attacks in Afghanistan, the people dying at Europe's borders and refugees getting wounded in the camps. 01/02/2021*

You miss me!

If I am far from your garden and bower
You miss me!
If I am far from your soil and land
You miss me!
If I am a butterfly around your candle
You miss me!
If I am tired and sick of you
You miss me!
If your soil is kohl of my eyes
You miss me!
If I am crying while missing you
You miss me!
If I read the history of your war to love you
You miss me!
If I read stories of your sky and land
You miss me!
If I am against you enemies with my pen
You miss me!
If I miss you over life and death borders
You miss me!

You miss me with your spring wind!
You miss me with an anemone flower!
You miss me with that ancient Herat!
You miss me with the pomegranate of Kandahar!
You miss me with Ghazni and Badakhshan!
You miss me with Kabul and Orozgan !
You miss me with garmet of creature!
You miss me with unity and solidarity!
You miss me if I am far from your embrace!
You miss me that I die being alone!
You miss me!
You miss me!

Author's Footnote: *Refugees must live far from their homeland for years. Afghanistan is my homeland, where I was born and grew up. I am missing Afghanistan often, and in this poem I recall the beauties of Afghanistan that I miss. 17/01/2021*

Like the light at the end of the tunnel

If there is no hope in the sky, you smile!
If the world does not let you sleep, you smile!
If the earth freezes you, shelter-less, you smile!
If the wind screams and frightens you, you smile!
Keep up your hope and smile!

Calm oceans follow the tsunamis
Sunny days succeed the rainy nights
Strong stones shape after volcano eruptions
Limpid water comes from deep wells
Like a light at the end of the tunnel, you smile!

Like a rainbow, after heavy storms
Like a revolution, after daring actions
Like a strong chain, after solidarity vows
Like a free bird, after breaking the chains
Keep your head up and smile

After standing against inequalities, you smile!
After asking for justice and what's right, you smile!
After fighting for peace against war, you smile!
After struggling for your future, you smile!
Make them afraid of your strength and smile!

Smile, as the world wants to wipe it!
Smile, as you find your life against it!
Smile, as you have solidarity behind yourself!
Smile, to burn the unjust eyes of the politicians!
Smile, as they are afraid to see you smiling!

Author's Footnote: *I believe that when there is no hope in our hearts, no light in our life and we have nothing to cure each other's pain, we can still give smiles as a gift to each other. Living the hardships of life as a refugee, I know that they will not take away the hope from my heart that comes with a smile. 08/01/2021*

Greetings to nature

Hey sun, warm my eyes
Through your broad bright rays
That can not be hidden by two hands
Hug me tight, don't leave me alone

Hey wind, sink into my hair
Through your vivid warm waves
That go among my long hair
Play with it under my scarf

Hey green fields, touch my knees
Through your sharp, tinny herbs
That kiss my hands, with peace
Lying down on you, let me rest

Hey sky, welcome my night
Through your smiling, sparkling stars
That decorated my tired mind
And soothed it with greetings from sunshines

Author's Footnote: *Just sitting on the grass, talking to nature from the depth of my heart, a moment where I am normal like other people, someone far from pains and traumas, somewhere on the grass at the northern part of the camp, together with my family, lying on the ground, and the sun touching my eyes.*

Butterfly and Nature

Tell them that she is fine
…Like the moon of midnight shine
Let them know that she will fly
…Over the mountain of hope in the sky

Silenced among drowned rights
…As through a hot crack on ice
Wishes for good night
…As roses disappearing in the light

Open our wings let's fly high
…Take a deep breath, let us cry
Pause is our death, let us go far
…Let's achieve what we are made for

Silence is spectator of their crimes
…Let's punish villains of the times
When harsh scenes come to mind
…The wilderness of humans make them blind

Let them know she was injured in war
…Once she was the rose of the desert
No more adorned and feathered
…Let us then mourn for her
Close this chapter, I am so tired!

Author's Footnote: *The two voices in this poem belong to me and to my historian friend Khpalwak. I am expressing my feelings as a refugee girl and he answers with messages of strength and resistance. 27/01/2021*

Up to Down

I see thousands of individuals
Who are stuck in a hell
Where demons are rulers
And liberation seekers criminals

Here is the world of wounded
Our injuries are not covered
Our tents are under rains
Our souls are dormant in pains

When the world wants to stop me
And the words want to sustain me
I get support from all those
That have stood behind me

I don't find depth in loudness
For the loudest words are not the deepest
I find my world in my words
And my words in my world

When we stand for our rights
You can imagine those nights
We slept hungry under tents
Far away, next to snowy mountains

If you are up and see us from above
Put yourself in our stead for once
Where we suffer you are able
To stand, to act for evacuation

Author's Footnote: *If only readers of this poem could view the wider world as if they were part of everything that happened in it; could listen to others and evaluate their decisions; could know that everyone is strong enough to make changes, find alternatives and prevent more people from sinking in the Tigris of hardships. 06/02/2021*

Now, it is you…and…they

You were so little, formed of blood
For nine months, she carried you
You were crying, you were yelling
With a warm hug, she enveloped you
She raised you and stayed with you

In the most critical moments
If she would have to choose
Your life or hers
She would wait, would hesitate
After a while, she would say
With a smile, it is "you"

Now, that she is gone, deep in the sky,
She watches you, she aids you
She admonishes: "stay strong"!
Focus your efforts, be the winner
Of this battle!
Now it is you …and…they

They who know endless pain in their veins
They who have no choice, no voice
Just orders they fear they must obey

If you are up and see them down
Hold their hands, help them be seen
Let them be heard through the world
With their own words!
That's what she wants to see you do

If life is short, keep this in mind:
Each action counts and past is past
Use your time, warm your heart
Stay on your path, don't feel unsafe
Life is a gamble, break the chains of doubt

We are all passengers of one train
Whose stations are uncertain
Those who now live under tents
With so much fear, so many worrying tears
Who lost their life, among these trails
Who are being killed in prisons

Take them away from freezing winds
Shelter them, with your heart
Share your love with compassion
Understand their repressed passion
For all those nights, they have tried so hard

Yes, now it is...I and...they.

Author's Footnote: Among the younger generation, many think that if peoples' ancestors were refugees and migrants from another country then they would not be so quick to judge those around them. The two voices in this poem are a boy and his grandma, and they describe the failing dreams of the boy's mother trying to find her child.. 17/03/2021

My body is covered, what about your eyes

I am not naked
If you cover your eyes
I am not weak
If you train your brain
Don't marry me for sex
If you have ex in your life

Don't punish me when
You can't achieve respect
Don't expect respect!
When you punish my sound

Don't cover me with pain. I know
You want to beat me, hurt me, shout at me
But you can't touch me or violate me
As there are strong united hands behind me

If the world wants to destroy me
Then my words will construct me
The world does not know the sense
Of being a mother, a sister
A girl, a wife among demons,
And still raise the sails for freedom

Author's Footnote: In the society we live in, our voices, our existence, and our abilities have stayed hidden but our body has been highlighted by the eyes and naked minds of men and sometimes even women. There are those among you who do not understand what it feels like to be a sister, a mother, a girl and a wife who has always sacrificed herself for her loved ones, but yet never able to defend her own rights. It comes with love and respect for women of my country who have been always forced to stay hidden and silent under Chadory yet who have nevertheless still been courageous to stay active and inspire. 28/03/2021

Don't look at me like that

Don't look at me like that!
I am not sad! I am not mad!
I am not bad! I am just tired!!
I need some more days to rest
Some more nights to sleep
Some more freedom to dream

I don't want to sleep late
Be the owl of midnight
I don't want to collapse on the table
Upon my books, without a blanket
One hand open under my cheek
The other closed tight around my pen
Writing even without seeing
Writing, in vain, our truth

I am very young
But my soul is very old
Don't look at me like that
I am not sad! I am not mad!
I am not bad! I am just tired

Author's Footnote: *In all my nights, my days, and my time trying to change my life for the better, I am not the only person, young girl or youth, who experiences these scenes and feels the expectations I have of society. No-one is on my side of things, instead I am plagued by many questions. 21/07/2021*

Carrying the Sun

Planets are on my crown
A big shiny, red star on the top
Mars, Jupiter and Venus
Like a circle round, round.

My hair is like the ocean,
One side cold and so rough,
Another, warm and calm.
This is the power of a woman.

My eyes are green leaves,
Dancing branches of a tree.
Its trunk is my neck,
Its roots form my shoulders.

These roots let my hands
Encircle the shining sun
That is heavy, red and bleeding
By human beings of the earth.

Author's Footnote: *We "women" control our feelings through the universe. Simply, each woman is a leader, in her family, in life, with all hardships she has and still is resistant. You are more than just beautiful. You are powerful, manager, organizer and leader. You can control the universe by opening your arms to yourself, loving and caring yourself, as you can find everything inside yourself. It is enough to think deeper, to feel your emotions more openly, and to start rebuilding yourself, if broken in the beginning, slowly but with resilience and strength.*